Marvelous Mabel

Figure Skating Superstar

by *Crystal Hubbard* ~ illustrated by *Alleanna Harris*

Lee & Low Books Inc.
New York

Giving up was never an option for Mabel Fairbanks. Born in Florida in 1915, Mabel was orphaned by the age of eight and bounced from home to home until an older brother in New York City agreed to take her in.

Sitting on the northbound train, Mabel watched as the poverty and confusion of life in the South grew distant and smaller. She fidgeted with excitement. Mabel knew something marvelous was waiting for her in New York City.

Mabel's brother and his wife owned a fish stand in Harlem.
"You're gonna have to work if you want to stay here," her sister-in-law demanded.

Mabel didn't mind the hard work and enjoyed talking to customers.

$0.25 $0.22 $0.15 $0.

Sometimes Mabel recognized the pain of a hungry tummy in other children and gave free fish to their mothers.

One day her sister-in-law caught her. "What are you doing?" she snapped.

"They were hungry," Mabel explained. "It's just one fish."

"They get what they can pay for," her sister-in-law insisted. "Don't do it again."

But Mabel kept giving fish away. Frustrated, Mabel's sister-in-law told her to leave the apartment. Her brother didn't say anything, so Mabel held her head high and walked out the door. But she had no place to go.

Mabel spent her days at school and took her meals at a church soup kitchen. When she couldn't sleep in a church, she spent her nights under a blanket of newspapers on a bench in Central Park.

Early one evening a young woman with a baby approached Mabel.
"Why are you sleeping in the park?" she asked.

"This is the only home I have now," Mabel answered.

"Well, you can't live out here," the woman said. "It's too cold and it isn't safe. I've been looking for someone to help with my baby. Would you come to my home and work for me?"

Eager for a roof other than branches with falling leaves, Mabel accepted.

Mabel slept in the nursery in the woman's apartment overlooking Central Park. She walked the baby through the park every day. Mabel often stopped to watch the skaters on the ice rink. The skaters glided in arcs, spins, and circles, never colliding, never stopping. Like wind-up toys, they danced over the ice.

That's so beautiful! Mabel thought. *I want to do that!*

One evening Mabel noticed a pair of big black skates in a pawnshop window. She entered the store and told the shopkeeper, "I'd like those skates, please."

The shopkeeper eyed Mabel. "If you've got the money, they're yours. Even though you could fit both your tiny feet in one skate."

"I'll give you fifty cents," she offered. "Those blades are so rusted and dull, they couldn't slice warm butter."

"Two dollars," the shopkeeper said.

"One dollar," Mabel said. "There's no line of folks waiting to buy those skates."

The shopkeeper grumbled. "Small price to be rid of you and the skates."

Mabel paid him and skipped home from the shop.

When Mabel tried on the skates, the shopkeeper's words came back to her: the skates were too big. They were also heavy, worn, and dark—not at all like the pretty snow-white boots of the skaters in Central Park.

Not one to give up, Mabel pulled out the cotton from an old stuffed toy and pushed it into the toes of the skates until they fit snugly. Mabel could now wear them . . . but she couldn't stand in them!

She found her balance by walking up and down the building's service stairwell, holding tightly to the railing.

Babies don't stay small for long, and soon Mabel's employers didn't need her anymore. The family sought the help of Wally Hunter, their building's part-time handyman, who was known for taking in homeless children. Everyone called him Uncle Wally. He gladly welcomed Mabel to his home.

Uncle Wally walked Mabel to school on his way to work at Schrafft's Ice Cream Company.

Every evening he prepared supper while Mabel completed her homework. For the first time in a long time, Mabel had someone to take care of her.

Mabel kept working on her balance in her oversized skates. Uncle Wally wrapped the blades in cardboard to protect the floors. Mabel clomped around the house, holding on to furniture until she found her footing.

Finally, Mabel was ready to try skating on ice. She went to a frozen pond in Morningside Park and quickly learned that even old skates with dull blades could move very fast.

Her feet stuttered across the blade-scarred ice.

Mabel fell.

She fell a lot, and she fell hard.

Sore and chilled, Mabel considered going home for the day
when a pair of skaters arrived. They studied the pond.
"Let's go to the Gay Blades rink," one of the girls suggested.
"The ice there is smooth and perfect."

Mabel quickly slipped out of her skates
and into her shoes. She followed the girls and stood
in line behind them at the entrance to the rink.

When it was Mabel's turn to pay the admission fee, the cashier refused the two quarters she offered him. "Uh-uh," he grunted. "Blacks don't skate here." He pointed to a sign posted on the wall.

Mabel wasn't surprised. There were lots of places she couldn't go because of her skin color. Frustration and disappointment hurt her far more than the falls at the pond.

Mabel returned to Morningside Park. She skated on the pond all winter until the ice began to vanish in the spring. She thought her chances to practice skating were disappearing as well.

But Uncle Wally had a clever plan. Using narrow pipes, sheets of tin, and wood planks, Uncle Wally fashioned a six-foot-by-six-foot square in Mabel's room. The sheets of tin sandwiched the pipes, and the wood planks held it all together.

Wearing a pair of work gloves, he carefully placed chunks of foggy white rocks in the pipes.

He took up a bucket of water. "Watch this. . . ." He poured a steady stream on the sheet of tin.

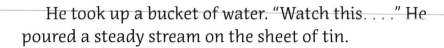

Mabel couldn't believe it—the water instantly froze!

"We use dry ice at the ice cream factory," Uncle Wally said. "It keeps our trucks cold so the ice cream doesn't melt when we make deliveries. Dry ice can freeze almost anything. When it melts, it evaporates. It's science."

No, Mabel thought. *It's magic!*

Mabel now had an ice rink with a surface as flawless as the one in Central Park, right in her very own room! She spent all her free time skating.

Mabel practiced on her right foot, tracing the figures she had seen other skaters execute. Once she perfected them, she practiced the same figures with her left foot. The rink was too small for long strides, so Mabel learned how to do sharp stops, turns, and whizzing spins of her own creation.

By the time winter returned, Mabel could perform short leaps and spins so fast, they left her dizzy and giggling. But she wanted more room to practice.

"I want to try to skate at the Gay Blades rink today," Mabel told Uncle Wally.

He handed Mabel a gift. "Take these with you. Maybe today will be your day."

Mabel rarely had anything brand-new, so she savored every second of opening her gift. A pair of white skates with shiny blades sat snug inside. She delighted in the smooth pearly leather, the blinding white laces, and the silver blades casting stars of light.

Mabel thanked Uncle Wally and rushed off to Gay Blades.

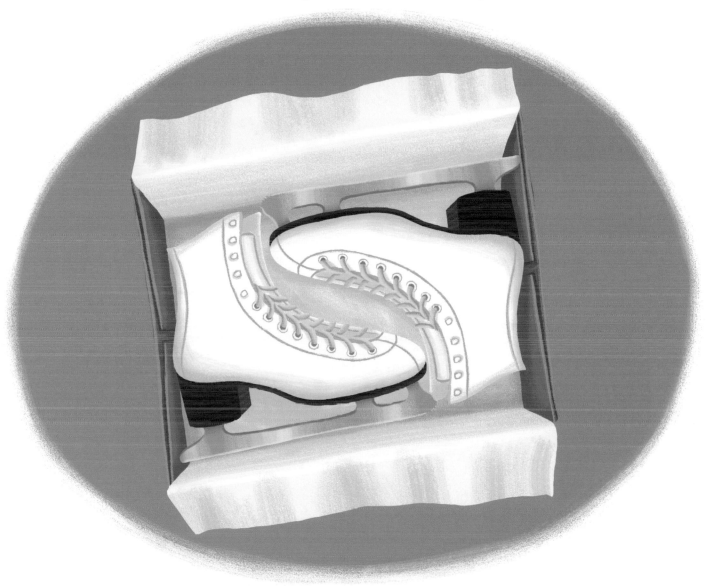

When she arrived at the rink, Mabel swallowed hard when she saw the manager, Lewis Clark, at the gate, but she stayed in line.

When it was her turn to pay, Mr. Clark opened his mouth to speak. Mabel got her words out first. "I would very much like to skate here," she said. "All I want to do is skate."

Mr. Clark turned to the cashier. "How long has she been trying to skate here?"

"Too long," Mabel and the cashier answered at the same time.

Mr. Clark chuckled. "Those are pretty skates. You sure you know what to do with them?"

"Let me onto the ice, and I'll show you," Mabel said.

He hesitated but eventually moved aside and allowed Mabel in the rink.

When Mabel stepped onto the ice, the other skaters stopped to stare at her. Scowling parents hauled their children off the rink. Disheartened, Mabel thought perhaps she should leave if other kids couldn't skate because of her.

She gazed upon the empty rink. This might be her first and only chance to skate the way she wanted. In her new white skates, Mabel glided farther onto the wide expanse of mirrored ice.

Arms extended wide, she caught the wind as she skated along the perimeter, gaining speed. She leaned forward until her right leg stretched behind her. *Skating isn't only like dancing.* Mabel smiled to herself. *It's like flying!*

She attempted a move she had seen others perform: a long leap from one foot to the other. She landed it solidly and then eased into a spin. Starting slowly with one knee raised, she brought her arms closer to her body, clasping her hands. Lowering her knee until one foot was crossed over the other and stretching her arms as high as she could, she spun until the world around her was a marvelous blur.

She threw out her arms, dug the toe of one skate into the ice, and came to an immediate stop, the tail of her coat swirling around her. Exhilaration rushed through Mabel! Skating as fast and as big as she wanted, she pushed off again, hoping her movements were as strong and graceful as those she'd first seen on the ice in Central Park.

"*I'm doing it!*" she thought joyously.

Mabel spent the rest of the afternoon skating. When it came time for her to go home, her joy sank into gloom.

If I'd never skated here, I'd never know what I was missing when I'm turned away tomorrow, she thought.

Lost in heartbreak, Mabel didn't notice Mr. Clark approach.

"I don't recall ever seeing anybody spin the way you do," he said. "Quite impressive. I guess I'll see you tomorrow."

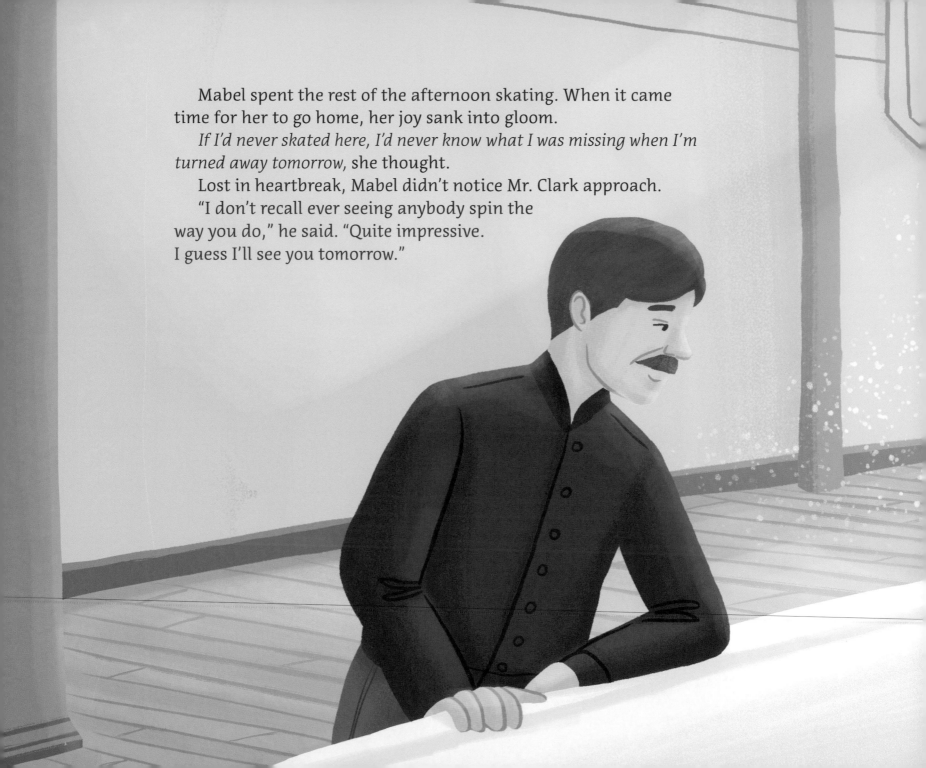

"I can come back?" Mabel asked in disbelief.

"I don't see why not." Mr. Clark said. "I'll make sure you get in any time you want to, Miss . . . ?"

"Mabel." She smiled and shook Mr. Clark's hand. "Thank you! When I came to New York City, I knew there was something special waiting for me. I'll keep practicing, and I'll become the most marvelous skater anyone has ever seen!"

Mabel skated as often as she could. She learned new skills by watching other skaters who worked with coaches. A couple of the coaches were so impressed that they taught Mabel for free after the rink closed.

When she got older, Mabel auditioned for professional skating shows. The companies refused to hire her because she was Black. So she did the next best thing: she created shows of her own and toured the United States, Mexico, and Cuba. In some of her shows, Mabel dazzled spectators by wearing lavish costumes and performing her incredible spins on a six-foot-by-six-foot rink. She became known as America's first Black figure skating star.

Mabel believed in sharing her passion for skating with others. After she retired from performing, she became a coach and helped students of all ages, races, and ethnicities to become champions.

"When I began skating, I was the only one out there fighting, and I had to fight that much harder. If I had been allowed to go to the Olympics or Ice Capades like I wanted to then, I may not have helped other Blacks like I did and coached such wonderful skaters. And I think all that has been just as important and meaningful."

—*Mabel Fairbanks*

Afterword

Despite her role as America's first Black figure skating star, Mabel Fairbanks never received much coverage by the mainstream press. As a result, the timeline and events in this book, and much of its dialogue (some imagined), were constructed from newspaper and magazine articles from the 1940s and 1950s, and a lengthy transcript of an interview that became public after Mabel's death.

Little information exists about Mabel's parents and early childhood, and much of that is conflicting. Mabel was born on November 14 or 15 in 1915 in Florida. Although Mabel stated her birthplace as the Florida Everglades, other sources report it was Jacksonville, Florida. When interviewed, Mabel gave her ancestry as African, English, and Seminole. Some sources report Mabel was sent to New York by kindly church members who rescued her from an abusive foster home. Others claim she went to New York in the company of brothers and sisters, with the intention of taking a secretarial course.

What is known for sure is that after her marvelous performance at the Gay Blades Ice Casino at Broadway and 52nd Street, Lewis Clark kept his word and allowed Mabel access to the ice. She caught the interest of two notable coaches: Howard Nicholson, who had coached three-time gold medalist Sonja Henie, and nine-time US Ladies Figure Skating champion Maribel Vinson-Owen. Recognizing her incredible natural talent, Nicholson and Vinson-Owen encouraged Mabel to perform in the fast, athletic, compact style she had mastered by skating on her dry-ice rink. Mabel also became adept at spirals, flying waltz jumps, spins, various "camel" spinning combinations, axel jumps, and quick stops.

By 1940, under Vinson-Owen's tutelage, Mabel had passed the tests of compulsory figures required by US Figure Skating (USFS) to compete in its sanctioned events. However, Mabel was not allowed to participate in USFS events, and this kept her out of the national and international competitions that might have given her the chance to compete in the Olympics.

When producers of the Ice Capades and Ice Follies wouldn't hire her because they were afraid audiences would walk out if they saw a Black skater, Mabel found jobs with smaller all-white companies that billed her as an "added attraction."

Wally Hunter became Mabel's manager and worked with Lewis Clark to create Mabel's first ice show, which took place at the Gay Blades Ice Casino on March 15, 1942. Her touring shows often included a six-foot-by-six-foot rink on which she amazed audiences with her speed and flexibility, and the tightness of her turns and spins. Mabel performed dynamic routines named "The Silver Spinning Top," "Dream Girl," "Dabbles on the Danube," "A Salute to Victory," and the "Swanee Snow Bird," an homage to her Florida origins. On May 5, 1945, *The Afro American* newspaper reviewed one of Mabel's shows and noted, "Particularly impressive was her 'Speed in Reverse' in which she skates backwards at breathless speed. Experts say she can skate backwards faster than most good skaters can forward."

In the early 1950s, Mabel went to Southern California, hoping to appear in one of Sonja Henie's productions. Afraid Mabel would upstage her with her unmatched jumps and spins, Henie refused to allow her in the show. The rejection crushed Mabel, but she turned that devastation into inspiration.

Mabel went on to guest star on *Frosty Frolics* with the show's headliner, Mae Edwards. She continued choreographing and staging successful shows of her own. When Mabel retired from performing, she settled in California and decided to become a coach. She had gained the respect of her colleagues but still faced racism from rink owners and skating organizations. After the Pasadena Figure Skating Club posted a sign stating "Colored trade not solicited," Mabel took law classes at Los Angeles Community College so she could fight the discriminatory practices of skating rinks and clubs.

Mabel then took her business to the Polar Palace in Hollywood. There, she built a roster of students that included celebrities such as Nat King Cole, Tab Hunter, Eartha Kitt, Dean Martin, Sammy Davis Jr., Frank Sinatra, and their children. Mabel taught anyone with a desire to skate, regardless of race or income. She never had children of her own, but she mothered her students. She let them sleep at her home in the Hollywood Hills to make sure they could get to practices. She used her own money to help them acquire costumes and skates, and she coached promising students for free if they couldn't afford lessons.

Her students included the first African Americans admitted to US Figure Skating clubs, Atoy Wilson and Richard Ewell III. Wilson became the first African American skater to win a national competition when he earned the gold medal in the US novice men's championship in 1966. Ewell partnered with Michelle McCladdie to become the first Black skaters to win the National Junior Pairs title in 1972.

Mabel had a special knack for creating Olympians. She paired Tai Babilonia and Randy Gardner as children. They grew up to capture five US pairs titles and the 1979 World Championship. Mabel also played a role in the development of Olympic gold medalists Scott Hamilton and Kristi Yamaguchi; US National champion and Olympic bronze medalist Debi Thomas (the first African American to win a Winter Olympic medal); US National champion and the first openly gay skater Rudy Galindo; and Tiffany Chin, who was the first Asian American to win a singles title at the US Championships.

When skaters and coaches created new moves, the skills were typically named after them. However, the variations of the basic spin first performed by Mabel do not bear her name. Her contribution to figure skating was finally recognized on February 14, 1997, when she became the first African American inducted into the US Figure Skating Hall of Fame, an honor bestowed on her for coaching. Mabel was inducted into the International Women's Sports Hall of Fame in 2001 and the Professional Skaters Association Hall of Fame in 2009.

On September 29, 2001, Mabel passed away of leukemia. Yet her trailblazing talent and work continue to ripple through the sport. In January 2021, the US Figure Skating Association introduced the Mabel Fairbanks Skatingly Yours Fund, established to provide support for the training and development of BIPOC (Black, Indigenous, People of Color) skaters. The fund is named for Mabel's habit of signing autographs with "Skatingly Yours." Team USA's Starr Andrews was the fund's inaugural recipient.

"Mabel Fairbanks' legacy of inclusiveness continues to be a lesson to us all," US Figure Skating president Anne Cammett said. "She helped lift and support a generation of Black, Latino, Indigenous, and Asian American skaters whose contributions in the sport continue today. This fund will continue her work while putting a much-needed spotlight on our athletes of color."

To Robin Washington, an extraordinary journalist and documentarian,
who taught me to chase good stories and haul them into the light —C. H.

To all the girls who kept going even though people told them no —A. H.

10 9 8 7 6 5 4 3 2 1
First Edition
Library of Congress Cataloging-in-Publication Data
Names: Hubbard, Crystal, author. | Harris, Alleanna, illustrator · Title: Marvelous Mabel: Figure Skating Superstar by Crystal Hubbard; illustrated by Alleanna Harris. Description: First Edition. | New York: Lee & Low Books Inc., [2022]Includes bibliographical references. Audience: Ages 6-9 years Audience: Grades 2-3 | Summary: "A picture book biography highlighting the early years of African American figure skater Mabel Fairbanks, who later became an Olympic coach and was inducted into the US Figure Skating Hall of Fame" Provided by publisher. Identifiers: LCCN 2021010246 | ISBN 9781620149560 (Hardcover) | ISBN 9781620149898 (ePub) · Subjects: LCSH: Fairbanks, Mabel, 1916-2001—Juvenile literature. | African American figure skaters—Biography—Juvenile literature. Skaters—United States—Biography—Juvenile literature. | Figure skating coaches—United States—Biography—Juvenile literature. | U.S. Figure Skating—History. | Discrimination in sports—United States—Juvenile literature. | Illustrated children's books. Classification: LCC GV850. F35 H84 2022 | DDC 796.91/2092 [B]-dc23 · LC record available at https://lccn.loc.gov/2021010246

Selected Bibliography

Afro Staff Correspondent. "Mabel Fairbanks Harrassed [sic] by Jim Crow." *The Afro American*, May 5, 1945. Accessed via https://news.google.com/newspapers?nid=2211&dat=19450505&id=TxOmAAAAIBAJ&pg=4076,4647016.

DeVerona, Donna. "Mabel Fairbanks and Breaking the Color Barrier in Figure Skating." ABC Sports. Shown during the 2003 US Figure Skating Nationals. YouTube video, May 30, 2011. https://www.youtube.com/watch?v=k-kW4bSdx2o.

Fairbanks, Mabel. "An Oral History: Mabel Fairbanks." Interview by Sharon Donnan. LA84 Foundation, 2018. https://digital.la84.org/digital/collection/p17103coll11/id/600/.

Farris, Jo Ann Schneider. *My Skating Life: Fifty Plus Years of Skating.* CreateSpace Independent Publishing Platform, 2016.

Gavilanes, Nancy. "A Pioneer at the Rink Is Proud of Her Legacy." *The New York Times*, January 14, 2001.

Greene, Marjorie E. "They Prepare for A New Nation." *Opportunity: Journal of Negro Life* XXI, no. 1 (1943): 74–76.

Griffin, Cynthia E. "Soul on Ice." *Our Weekly Los Angeles*, January 27, 2010. http://ourweekly.com/news/2010/jan/27/soul-on-ice/.

Honey, Maureen, ed. *Bitter Fruit: African American Women in World War II.* Columbia, MO: University of Missouri Press, 1999.

LA84 Foundation. "Skating For Her Moment: The Mabel Fairbanks Story." January 30, 2019. https://la84.org/skating-for-her-moment-the-mabel-fairbanks-story/.

Levine, Bettijane. "The Ice Mother Blazed the Skating Trail for Others." *Los Angeles Times*, February 19, 1998.

Miller, Buster. "Time Out . . ." *The New York Age*, May 9, 1942.

Runstedtler, Theresa. "From White Wash to Black Ice: Black Athletes in Unexpected Places." *Journal of American Ethnic History*, 35, no. 2 (Winter 2016): 79–90.

Stevens, Ryan. "I've Cried Enough For All of Us: The Mabel Fairbanks Story." *Skate Guard*, March 26, 2015. http://skateguard1.blogspot.com/2015/03/ive-cried-enough-for-all-of-us-mabel.html.

US Figure Skating Fan Zone. "Mabel Fairbanks Skatingly Yours Fund Established to Support BIPOC Skaters." January 15, 2021. https://usfigureskatingfanzone.com/news/2021/1/15/figure-skating-mabel-fairbanks-skatingly-yours-fund-established-to-support-bipoc-skaters.aspx